How I Carried the Message to Garcia

By Andrew Summer Rowan

Layout and Cover Copyright ©2010
All Rights Reserved
Printed in the USA

Published by ReadaClassic.com
ISBN#: 9781611044140

Table of Contents

How I Carried the Letter to Garcia 5

Footnotes 41

"Let us both small and great push forward in this work, in this pursuit, if to our country, if to ourselves we would live dear."

— Horace

How I Carried the Letter to Garcia

"Where," asked President McKinley of Colonel Arthur Wagner, head of the Bureau of Military Intelligence, "where can I find a man who will carry a message to Garcia?"

The reply was prompt. "There is a young officer here in Washington; a lieutenant named Rowan, who will carry it for you !"

"Send him!" was the President's order.

The United States faced a war with Spain. The President was anxious for information. He realized that success meant that the soldiers of the republic must cooperate with the insurgent forces of Cuba. He understood that it was essential to know how many Spanish troops there were on the island, their quality and condition, their morale, the character of their officers, especially those of the high command; the state of the roads in all seasons; the sanitary situation in both the Spanish and insurgent armies and the country in general; how well both sides were armed and what the Cuban forces would need in order to harass the enemy while American battalions were being mobilized; the topography of the country and many other important facts.

Small wonder that the command, "Send him!" was equally as prompt as the answer to his question respecting the individual who would carry the message to Garcia.

It was perhaps an hour later, at noon, when Colonel Wagner came to me to ask me to meet him at the Army and Navy Club for lunch at one o'clock. As we were eating, the colonel – who had, by the way, a reputation for being an inveterate joker – asked me: "When does the next boat leave for Jamaica?"

Thinking he was making an effort to perpetrate one of his pleasantries, and determined to thwart him, if possible, I excused myself for a minute or so and when I had returned informed him that the "Adirondack," of the Atlas Line, a British boat, would sail from New York the next day at noon.

"Can you take that boat?" snapped the colonel.

Notwithstanding that I still believed the colonel was joking I replied in the affirmative.

"Then," said my superior, "get ready to take it!"

"Young man," he continued, "you have been selected by the President to communicate with – or rather, to carry a message to – General Garcia, who will be found somewhere in the eastern part of Cuba. Your problem will be to secure from him information of a military character, bring it down to date and arrange it on a working basis. Your message to him will be in the nature of a series of inquiries from the President. Written communication, further than is necessary to identify you, will be avoided. History has furnished us with the record of too many tragedies to warrant taking risks. Nathan Hale of the Continental Army, and Lieutenant Richey in the War with Mexico were both caught with dispatches; both were put to death and in the case of the latter the plans for Scott's invasion of Vera Cruz was divulged to the enemy. There must be no failure on your part; there must be no errors made in this case."

By this time I was fully alive to the fact that Colonel Wagner was not joking.

"Means will be found," he continued, "to identify you in Jamaica, where there is a Cuban junta. The rest depends on you. You require no further instructions than those I will now give you." which he did, they being essentially as outlined in the opening paragraphs. "You will need the afternoon for preparation. Quarter-master-General Humphreys will see that you are put ashore at Kingston. After that, providing the United States declares war on Spain, further instructions will be based on cables received from you. Otherwise everything will be silence. You must plan and act for yourself. The task is yours and yours only. You must get a message to Garcia. Your train leaves at midnight. Good-by and good luck!"

We shook hands.

As Colonel Wagner released mine he repeated: "Get that message to Garcia!"

Hastily, as I set about to make my preparations, I considered my situation. My duty was, as I understood it, complicated by the fact that a state of war did not exist, nor would it exist at the time of my departure; possibly not until after my arrival in Jamaica. A false step might bring about a condition that a lifetime of statement would never explain. Should war be declared my mission would be simplified, although its dangers would not be lessened.

In instances of this kind, where one's reputation, as well as his life, is at stake, it is usual to ask for written instructions. In military service the life of the man is at the disposal of his country, but his reputation is his own and it ought not be placed in the hands of anyone with power to destroy it, either by neglect or otherwise. But in this case it never occurred to me to ask for written instructions; my sole thought was that I was charged with a message to Garcia and to get from him certain information and that I was going to do it.

Whether Colonel Wagner ever placed on file in the office of the adjutant-general the substance of our conversation I do not know. At this late day it matters little.

My train left Washington at 12:01 a.m., and I have a recollection of thinking of an old superstition about starting on a journey on Friday. It was Saturday when the train departed, but it was Friday when I left the club. I assumed the Fates would decide that I had left on Friday. But I soon forgot that in my mental discussion of other matters and did not recall it until some time afterward and then it mattered nothing, for my mission had been completed.

The "Adirondack" left on time and the voyage was without special incident. I held myself aloof from the other passengers and learned only from a traveling companion, an electrical engineer, what was going on. He conveyed to me the cheerful information that because of my keeping away from them and giving no one any information as to my business, a bunch of convivial spirits had conferred on me the title of "the bunco steerer."

It was when the ship entered Cuban waters that I first realized danger. I had but one incriminating paper, a letter from the State Department to officials in Jamaica saying that I was what I might represent myself to be. But if war had been declared before the Adirondack entered Cuban waters she would have been liable to search by Spain, under the rules of international law. As I was contraband and the bearer of contraband I could have been seized as a prisoner of war and taken aboard any Spanish ship, while the British boat, after compliance with specified preliminaries, could have been sunk, despite the fact that she left a peaceful port under a neutral flag, bound for a neutral port, prior to a declaration of war.

Recalling this state of affairs, I hid this paper in the life preserver in my stateroom and it was with great relief I saw the cape astern.

By nine the next morning I had landed and was a guest of Jamaica. I was soon in touch with Mr. Lay, head of the

Cuban junta, and with him and his aids planning to get to Garcia as soon as possible.

I had left Washington April 8-9. April 20 the cables announced that the United States had given Spain until the 23 to agree to surrender Cuba to the Cubans and to withdraw her armed forces from the island and her navy from its waters. I had in cypher cabled my arrival and on April 23 a reply in code came: "Join Garcia as soon as possible!"

In a few minutes after its receipt I was at headquarters of the junta, where I was expected. There were a number of exiled Cubans present whom I had not met before and we were conversing on general topics when a carriage drove up.

"It is time!" someone exclaimed in Spanish. Following which, without further discussion, I was led to the vehicle and took a seat inside.

Then began one of the strangest rides ever taken by a soldier on duty or off. My driver proved to be the most taciturn of Jehus. He spoke not to me, nor heeded me when I spoke to him. The instant I was shut in he started through the maze of Kingston's streets at a furious pace. On and on he drove, never slackening speed, and soon we had passed the suburbs and were beyond all habitations. I knocked, yes, kicked, but he gave no heed.

He seemed to understand that I was carrying a message to Garcia and that it was his part to get me over the first "leg" of the journey as speedily as possible. So, after several futile efforts to make him listen to me, I

How I Carried the Letter to Garcia

decided to let matters take their course and settled back in my seat.

Four miles farther, through a dense growth of tropical trees, we flew along the broad and level Spanish Town road, until at the edge of the jungle we halted, the door of the cab was opened, a strange face appeared, and I was invited to transfer to another carriage that was waiting.

But the strangeness of it all! The order in which everything appeared to be arranged! Not an unnecessary word was indulged in, not a second of time was wasted.

A minute later and again I was on my way.

The second driver, like the first, was dumb. He declined all efforts made to get him in conversation, contenting himself by putting his horses to as swift a pace as possible, so on we went through Spanish Town and up the valley of the Cobre river to the backbone of the island where the road runs down to the ultramarine waters of the Caribbean at St. Ann's Bay.

Still not a word from my driver, although I repeatedly endeavored to get him to talk to me. Not a sound, not a sign that he understood me: just a race along a splendid road, breathing more freely as the altitude increased, until as the sun set we drew up beside a railway station.

But what is this mass of ebony rolling down the slope of the cut toward me? Had the Spanish authorities anticipated me and placed Jamaica officers on my trail? I was uneasy for a monument as this apparition came in sight, but relief came when an old Negro hobbled to the carriage and shoved through the door a deliciously fried chicken and two bottles of Bass' ale, at the same time letting loose a volley of dialect, which, as I was able to catch a word here and there, I understood was highly complementary to me for helping Cuba gain her freedom and giving me to understand that he was "doing his bit" with me.

But my driver stood not on ceremony, nor was he interested in either chicken or conversation. In a trice a new pair of horses was relayed on and away we went my Jehu plying his whip vigorously. I had only time enough to thank the old Negro by shouting: "Good-by, Uncle!"

In another minute we had left him and were racing through the darkness at breakneck speed.

Although I fully comprehended the gravity and importance of the errand in which I was engaged, I lost sight of it for the time in my admiration of the tropical forests. these wear their beauty at night as well as by day. The difference is that while during the sunlight it is the vegetable world that is in perennial bloom, at night it is the insect world in its flight that excites attention. Hardly had the short twilight changed to utter darkness when the glowworms turned on their phosphorescent lights and flooded the woods with their weird beauties. These magnificent fireflies illuminated with their incandescence the forest I was traversing until it resembled a veritable fairyland.

But even such wonders as these are forgotten in the recollection of duty to be performed. We still coursed onward at a speed that was limited only by the physical

How I Carried the Letter to Garcia

abilities of the horses, when suddenly a shrill whistle sounded from the jungle!

My carriage stopped. Men appeared as if they had sprung from the ground. I was surrounded by a party of men armed to the teeth. I had no fear of being intercepted on British soil by Spanish soldiers, but these abrupt halts were getting on my nerves, because action by the Jamaica authorities would mean the failure of the mission, and if the Jamaica authorities had been notified that I was violating the neutrality of the island I would not be allowed to proceed. What if these men were English soldiers!

But my feelings were soon relieved. A whispered parley and we were away again!

In about an hour we halted in front of a house outlined by feeble lights within. Supper waited. The junta manifestly believed in liberal feeding.

The first thing offered me was a glass of Jamaica rum. I do not recall that I was tired, although we had traveled about seventy miles in approximately nine hours with two relays, but I do know that the rum was welcome.

Following came introductions. From an adjoining room came a tall, wiry, determined-looking man, with a fierce moustache, one of his hands minus a thumb; a man to tie to in an emergency, to trust at any time. His eyes were honest, loyal eyes that mirrored a noble soul. He was a Peninsula Spaniard who had gone to Cuba, at Santiago had quarreled with the rule of Old Spain, hence the missing thumb and exile. He was Gervacio Sabio and he was charged with seeing that I was guided to General Garcia for the delivery of my message. The others were the men employed to get me out of Jamaica – seven miles remaining to be traveled – with one exception, one man was to be my "assistente," or orderly.

Following a rest of an hour we proceeded. Half an hour's travel from the hut we were again halted by whistle signals. We alighted and entered a cane field through which we tramped in silence for about a mile until we came to a coconut grove bordering a plaything of a bay.

Fifty yards off shore a small fishing boat rocked softly on the water. Suddenly a light flashed aboard the little craft. It must have been a time signal, for our arrival had been noiseless. Gervacio, apparently satisfied with the alertness of the crew, answered it.

Following some conversation during which I thanked the agents of the junta, I climbed on the back of one of the boat's crew who had waded ashore and was carried to the boat.

I had completed the first part of the journey to Garcia.

Once aboard the boat I noted that it was partially filled with boulders intended for ballast. Oblong bundles indicated cargo, but not sufficient to impede progress. But with Gervacio as skipper, the crew of two men, my assinstente and myself, the boulders and the bundles, there was little room for comfort.

I indicated to Gervacio my desire to get beyond the three-mile limit as soon as possible, as I did not want to impose upon the hospitality of Great Britain longer than necessary. He replied that the boat would have to be rowed beyond the head lands, as there was not sufficient wind in the small bay to fill her sails. We were soon outside the cape, however, our sails caught the breeze and the second stretch of the trip to the strife-torn objective was begun.

I have no hesitation in saying that there were some anxious moments for me following our departure. My reputation was at stake if I should be caught within the three-mile limit off the Jamaica coast. My life would be at stake if I should be caught within three miles of the Cuban coast. My only friends were the crew and the Caribbean sea.

One hundred miles to the north lay the shores of Cuba, patrolled by Spanish "lanchas," light-draft vessels armed with pivot guns of small caliber, and machine guns, their crews provided with Mauser rifles, far superior – as I afterward learned – to anything we had aboard; as motley a collection of small arms as could be picked up anywhere. In the event of an encounter with one of these "lanchas" there was little to hope for.

But I must succeed; I must find Garcia and deliver my message!

Our plan of action was to keep outside the Cuban three-mile limit until after sunset, then to sail or row in rapidly, draw behind some friendly coral reef and wait until morning. If we were caught, as we carried no papers, we would probably be sunk and no questions asked. Boulder-laden craft go to the bottom quickly and floating bodies tell no tales to those who find them.

It was now early morning, the air was deliciously cool and, wearied with my journey thus far I was about to seek some rest in sleep when suddenly Gervacio gave an exclamation that brought us all to our feet. A few miles away one of the dreaded lanchas was bearing directly toward us.

A sharp command in Spanish and the crew dropped the sail.

Another and all save Gervacio, who was at the helm, were below the gun wale, and he was lounging over the tiller, keeping the boat's nose parallel with the Jamaica shore.

"He may think I am a 'lone fisherman" from Jamaica and go by us," said the cool-headed steersman.

So it proved. When within hailing distance the pert young commander of the lancha cried in Spanish: "Catching anything?"

To which my guide responded, also in Spanish: "No, the miserable fish are not biting this morning!"

If only that midshipman, or whatever his rank, had been wise enough to lay alongside, he surely would have "caught something," and this story would never have been written. When he had passed us and was some distance away, Gervacio ordered sail hoisted again and turning to me remarked: "If the Senor is tired and wants sleep, he can now indulge himself, for I think the danger is past."

If anything occurred during the next six hours, it left me undisturbed. In fact, I believed that nothing except the broiling heat of the tropical sun could have drawn me from my rocky mattress. But it did for the Cubans, who were quite proud of their English greeted me with: "Buenos dias, Meester Rowan!" The sun shone brilliantly all day. Jamaica was all aglow, like some mighty jewel in a setting of emerald. The turquoise sky was cloudless and to the south the green slopes of the island were blocked off in large squares, showing to great advantage the light verdancy of the cane fields alternating with the deeper hue of the forests. It was a splendid and a magnificent picture. But northward all was gloom. An immense bank of clouds enshrouded Cuba and, watch as keenly as we might, we saw no sign of their lifting. But the wind held true and even increased in volume during the hours. We were making good progress and Gervacio at the tiller was happy, joking with the crew and smoking like a "fumarole."

About four o'clock in the afternoon the clouds broke away and the Sierra Maestra, the master mountain range of the island, stood in the golden sunshine in all its beauteous majesty. It was like drawing the curtain aside and placing on view a matchless picture by an artist monarch. Here were color, mass, mountain, land and sea blended in one splendid ensemble, the like of which is found nowhere else, for there is no place on earth where a mountain height of 8000 feet, its summits clothed in verdure and its great battlements extending for hundreds of miles!

But my admiration was short lived. Gervacio broke the spell when he began taking in sail. To my question he replied: "We are closer than I thought. We are in the war zone of the lanchas, high seas or no high seas. We must stand well out and use the open water for all it is worth. To go closer and run the risk of being seen by the enemy is merely to run an unnecessary risk."

Hastily we overhauled the arsenal. I carried only a Smith & Wesson revolver, so I was assigned a frightful looking rifle. I might have been able to fire it once, but I doubt if it would have been of further service. The crew and my assistente were provided with the same formidable weapons, while the pilot, who from his seat looked after the jib, the only sail set, drew close to him the other weapons. The real serious part of my mission was now at hand. Hitherto everything had been easy and comparatively safe. Now danger menaced. Grave danger. Capture meant death and my failure to carry my message to Garcia.

We were probably twenty-five miles from the coast, although it seemed but a span away. It was not until nearly midnight that the jib-sheet was let go and the crew began sounding the shallow water with their oars. Then a timely roller gave us a last lift and with a mighty effort shoved us into the waters of a hidden peaceful bay. We anchored in the darkness fifty yards off shore. I suggested that we land at once, but Gervacio replied:

"We have enemies both ashore and afloat, Senor; it is better that we stay where we are. Should any lancha endeavor to pry us out she would likely land on the submerged coral reef we have crossed and we can get ashore, and from the obscurity of the grape entanglements we can play the game."

The tropical haze which ever hangs mist like at the meeting of the sea and sky in low altitudes began to lift slowly, disclosing a mass of grape, mangrove thickets and thorn-set trees, reaching almost to the edge of the water. It was difficult to perceive objects with distinctness, but as if declining to puzzle us further as to the nature of our surroundings, the sun rose gloriously over El Turquino, the highest point in all Cuba. In an instant everything had changed, the mist had vanished, the darkness of the low-lying thicket against the mountain wall had been dissipated, the gray of the water breaking against the shore had been transformed as if by magic to a marvelous green. It was one splendid triumph of light over darkness.

Already the crew were busy transferring luggage ashore. Noting me standing mute and seemingly dazed, for I was thinking of the lines by a poet who must have had a similar scene in mind when he wrote: "Night's candles are burnt out and jocund day stands tiptoe on the misty mountain tops," Gervacio said in a low tone to me: "El Turquino, Senor" — the Tutor.

As I stood there drinking in the glory of that marvelous morning, little did I dream that I was standing within a stone's throw, almost, of what was soon to be the watery sepulcher of the mighty "Colon," a great battleship, then first in her class and bearing the name of the greatest of all admirals, Christopher Columbus, the discoverer of America, this great ship having already been selected by the Fates to be destroyed by our own warships in the sea fight off Santiago.

But my reveries were soon ended. The freight was landed, I was carried ashore, the boat dragged to a small estuary, overturned and hidden in the jungle. By this time a number of ragged Cubans had assembled at our landing place. Where they came from, or how they knew that our party was a friendly one, were problems too deep for me. Signals of some sort had doubtless been exchanged and they had come to act as burden-bearers. Some of them had seen service, some of them bore the marks made by Mauser bullets.

Our landing place seemed to be a junction of paths running in all directions away from the coast and into the thicket. Off to the west, seemingly about a mile away, little columns of smoke were rising through the vegetation. I learned that this smoke was from a "salina," or pan where salt was being made for the refugee Cubans who had hidden in these mountains after fleeing from the dreaded concentration camps.

The second "leg" of the journey was completed.

Hitherto there had been danger; from this time on there would be more. Spanish troops mercilessly hunted down Cubans and small mercy was shown by the forces directed by Weyler, the "butcher," to men found in arms, or outside the concentration camps, even though they might be unarmed. The remainder of the journey to Garcia was fraught with many dangers and I knew it, but this was no time to consider them; I must be on my way!

The topography of the country was simple enough; a level strip of land extending a mile or so inland toward the north, covered with jungle. Man's handiwork had been confined to cutting paths, and the network could be threaded only by the Cubans reared in this labyrinth. The heat soon became oppressive and caused me to envy my companions, none of whom were burdened by superfluous clothing.

Soon we were on the march, screened from the sea and the mountains, and indeed, from each other, by the denseness of the foliage, the twists and turns of the trail and the torrid haze that soon settled over everything. The jungle was converted into a miniature inferno by the sun, although we could not see it through the verdure. But as we left the coast and approached the foothills the jungle began to give way to a larger and less dense growth. We soon reached a clearing where we found a few bearing coconut trees. The water fresh and cool, drawn from the nuts, was elixir to our parched throats.

But not long did we tarry in this pleasant spot. A march of miles lay before us and a climb up steep mountain slopes to another hidden clearing must be made before nightfall. Soon we had entered the true tropical forest. Here traveling was somewhat easier, for a current of air, hardly perceptible, but a current of air nevertheless, made breathing less of a task and, by far, more refreshing.

Through this forest runs the "Royal Road" from Portillo to Santiago de Cuba. As we neared this highway I noted my companions one by one disappearing in the jungle. I was soon left alone with Gervacio. Turning to him to ask a question I saw him place a finger on his lips, mutely sign to me to have my rifle and revolver in readiness and then he too vanished amid the tropical growth.

I was not long in ascertaining the reason for this strange conduct. The jingle of horses' trappings, the rattling of the short sabers carried by Spanish cavalry and occasionally a word of command, fell on my ear.

But for the vigilance of those with me we should have walked out on the highway just in time to encounter a hostile force!

I cocked my rifle and swung my Smith & Wesson into position for quick action and waited tensely for what was to follow. Every moment I expected to hear reports of firearms. But none came and one by one the men returned, Gervacio being among the last.

"We scattered in order to deceive them in the event we had been discovered. We covered a considerable stretch of the road and had firing been commenced the enemy would have believed it an attack in force from ambush. It would have been a successful one too," Gervacio added with an expression of regret, "but duty first and," – here he smiled – "pleasure afterward!"

Beside the trails along which insurgent parties usually passed, it was the custom to build fires and bury sweet potatoes in the ashes. There they roasted until a hungry party should pass. We came upon one of these fires during the afternoon. A baked sweet potato was passed out to each of the party, the fire covered again and the march resumed.

As we ate our sweet potatoes I thought of Marion and his men in the days of the revolution, who fought their battles on a like diet, and through my mind flashed the idea that as Marion and his men had fought to victory, so also would these Cubans, who were inspired by a desire for liberty similar to that actuating the patriot fathers of my own country, and it was with a feeling of pride that I recalled that my mission was to aid these people in their efforts by communicating with their general and making it possible for the soldiers of my nation to do battle in their behalf.

Arriving at the end of the journey for the day, I observed a number of men in a dress strange to me.

"Who are these?" I inquired.

"They are deserters from the army of Spain, Senor," replied Gervacio. "They have fled from Manzanillo and they say that lack of food and harsh treatment by their officers were the reasons for their leaving."

Now a deserter is sometimes of value, but here in this

wilderness I would have preferred their room to their company. Who could say that one or more of them might not leave camp at any time and warn the Spanish officials that an American was crossing Cuba, evidently bound for the camp of General Garcia? Would not the enemy make every effort to thwart him in his mission? So I said to Gervacio: "Question these men closely and see that they do not leave camp during our stay!"

"Si, Senor!" was the reply.

Well for me and the success of my errand that I had give out such instruction. My thought that one or more deserters might leave to apprise the Spanish commander of my presence proved to be the correct one. Although it is not fair to presume that any knew my mission, my being there was sufficient to arouse the suspicions of two who proved to be spies and also nearly resulted in my assassination. These two determined to leave camp that night and plunge through the thickets to the Spanish lines with the information that an "officer Americano" was being escorted across Cuba.

I was awakened sometime after midnight by the challenge of a sentinel, followed by a shot, and almost instantly a shadowy form appeared close by my hammock. I sprang up and out on the opposite side just as another form appeared and in less time than it takes to write it the first one had fallen as the result of a blow from a machete, which cut through the bones of his right shoulder to the lung. The wretch lived long enough to tell us that it was agreed if his comrade failed to get out of camp, he should kill me and prevent the carrying out of whatever project I was engaged in. The sentinel shot and killed his comrade.

Horses and saddles were not available until late next day, at an hour that made it impossible to proceed. I chafed at the delay, but it could not be helped. Saddles were harder to secure than horses. I was somewhat impatient and asked Gervacio why we could not proceed without saddles.

"General Garcia is besieging Bayamo, in Central Cuba, Senor," was his reply, "and we shall have to travel a considerable distance in order to reach him."

This was the reason for the search for "monturas," the saddles and trappings. One look at the steed assigned me and my admiration for the wisdom of my guide mounted rapidly and increased noticeably during the four days' ride. Had I ridden that skeleton without a saddle it would have meant exquisite torture. However, I will say for the horse, that with his "montura" he proved a mettlesome beast, far superior to many a well-fed horse of the plains of America.

Our trail followed the backbone of the ridge for some distance after leaving camp. One unaccustomed to these trails must surely have been driven desperate by the perplexity of the wilderness, but our guides seemed to be as familiar with the tortuous windings as they would have been on a broad high road.

Shortly after we had left the divide and had begun the descent of the eastern slope we were greeted by a motley assembly of children and an old man whose white hair streamed down his shoulders. The column halted, a few words passed between the patriarch and Gervacio, and then the forest rang with "Vivas," for the United States, for Cuba and the "Delegado Americano." It was a touching incident. How they had learned of my approach I never knew; but news travels fast in the jungle and my arrival had made one old man and a crowd of little children happier.

At Yara, where the river leaves the foothills we camped that night, it was brought to me that we were in a zone where danger lurked. "Trincheras" or trenches had been built to defend the gorge should the Spanish columns march out from Manzanillo. Yara is a great name in Cuban history, for from the town of Yara came the first cry for "liberty" in the "Ten Years' War" of 1868-78. I was asked to swing my hammock behind the trinchera, which, by the way, was not a trench at all, but a breast-high wall of stones, and I noticed that a guard, recruited from some unknown source, was posted and kept on duty all night.

Gervacio intended taking no chances on my mission being a failure.

Next morning we began the ascent of the spur projecting northward from the Sierra Maestra, forming the east bank of the river. Our course lay across the eroded ridges. Danger lurked in the lowlands. There was the possibility of ambuscade, fire and the chance of being cut off by some mobile party of Spaniards.

Here began a series of ups and downs across the streams with vertical banks. In my career I have seen much cruelty to animals, but never anything to equal this. To get the poor horses down to the bottom of these gulches and out again involved forms of punishment beyond belief. But there was no help for it; the message to Garcia must be delivered, and in war what are the sufferings of a few horses when the freedom of hundreds of thousands of human beings is at stake? I felt sorry for the brutes, but this was no time for sentiment.

It was with great relief that after the hardest day of riding I had ever experienced we halted at a hut in the midst of corn patches near the edges of the forest, at Jibaro. A freshly killed beef was hanging to the rafters, while the cook in the open was busy preparing a meal for the "Delegado Americano." My coming had been heralded and my feast was to consist of fresh beef and cassava bread.

Hardly had I finished my generous meal when a great commotion was heard, voices and the clatter of horses' hoofs at the edge of the forest. Colonel Castillo of the staff of General Rios had arrived. He welcomed me in the name of his chief, who was due to arrive in the morning, with all the grace of a trained staff officer; then mounting his steed with an athletic spring, put the spurs to his mount in frenzied fashion and was off, as he came, like a flash. His welcome assured me that I was making headway under a skillful guide.

General Rios came next morning and with him Colonel Castillo, who presented me with a Panama hat "made in Cuba." General Rios was "the general of the coasts." He was very dark, evidently of Indian and Spanish blood, with springy, athletic step. No Spanish column ever made a sortie in his district and found him unprepared. His sources of information and his intuition were uncanny. It was no small task to move hiding families and provide for their maintenance, but he did it and, as may be supposed, advance information of enemy movements was imperative. The Spanish methods were to enter the forests, scour them and, in default of prey, lay the districts in waste. Meanwhile General Rios would conduct matters in guerilla fashion and his forces were continuously taking pot shots at the Spanish columns, sometimes doing terrible execution.

General Rios added two hundred cavalrymen to my escort. As we marched single file we would have presented a formidable appearance had there been anyone to see us.

I could not help observing that we were being led with remarkable skill and speed. We had entered the forest again and were hiding in the evergreen dress of the Sierra Maestra. The trail was comparatively level, but crossed at intervals by water courses with steep banks. The paths were so narrow we were constantly running afoul of tree trunks, barking our shins and dislodging the impedimenta from the backs of our horses. Still the guide held to a steady gait that caused me to marvel. My usual position was near the center of the column, but I wanted to be near this centaur who was in the lead and at the next water course crossing I rode forward to observe him. He was a coal black Negro, Dionisito Lopez, a lieutenant in the Cuban army. He could trace a course through this trackless forest, through the tangled growth, as fast as he could ride. His skill with a machete was amazing. He carved a way for us through the jungle. Networks of vines fell before his steady strokes right and left; closed spaces became openings; the man appeared tireless.

The night of April 30 brought us to the Rio Buey, an affluent of the Bayamo River, and about twenty miles from the city of Bayamo. Our hammocks had scarcely been swung when Gervacio appeared, his face aglow with satisfaction.

"He is there, Senor! General Garcia is in Bayamo and the Spaniards are in retreat down the Cauto river. Their rear-guard is at Cauto-El-Embarcadero!"

So eager was I to get in communication with Garcia that I proposed a night ride, but after a conference it was decided that nothing would be gained.

May-day, 1898, is "Dewey Day" in our calendar. As I was sleeping in the forests of Cuba, the great admiral was feeling his way past the guns of Corregidor into Manila Bay to destroy the Spanish fleet. While I was on my way to Garcia that day he had sunk the Spanish ships and with his guns was menacing the capital of the Philippines.

Early that morning we were on our way. Terrace by

terrace we descended the slope leading to the plain of Bayamo. This great stretch of country, laid waste for years, was now as if man had never been. At the black remnant of the hacienda of Candalaria, mute evidence of Spanish methods of warfare, we passed into the plain. We had ridden more than one hundred miles through a wilderness with hardly a habitation to show that man had ever lived in one of Nature's most favored spots across a tropical garden gone to weeds. Through grass so high that our column was hidden from sight, through burning sun and blistering heat, we traveled, but all our discomforts were forgotten in the thought that our destination was at hand; our mission nearly ended. Even our jaded horses seemed to share in our anticipation and eagerness.

At the erstwhile Peralejo, the scene of the attack by Maceo on the column of General Campos, we struck the royal road to Manzanillo-Bayamo and encountered joyous human beings in rags and tatters, all hurrying toward the town. The chatter of these happy groups reminded me of the parrots that had shrieked at our passage through the jungles. They were going back to the homes from which they had been driven.

It was but a short ride from Paralejo to the banks of the eastern side of the river to the town, once a city of 30,000, now a mere village of perhaps 2000. It was surrounded by a row of blockhouses the Spaniards had built on both sides of the stream. These little forts were the first objects to be seen and their prominence was emphasized by the flames and smoke still rising as we came into view. The Cubans had set them on fire when they entered the former metropolis of these once flourishing valley.

We soon lined up on the bank, and after Gervacio and Lopez had talked to the guards, we proceeded. We halted in midstream to allow our horses to drink and to store up a little energy for our final dash into the presence of the officer in charge of Cuba's military destiny east of the Jucaro-Moron trocha.[1]

In a few minutes I was in the presence of General Garcia.

The long and toilsome journey with its many risks, its chances of failure, its chances for death, was over.

I had succeeded.

As we arrived in front of General Garcia's headquarters the Cuban flag was hanging lazily over the door from an inclined staff. The method of reaching the presence of a man to whom one is accredited in such circumstances was new to me. We formed in line, dismounted together, and "stood to horse." Gervacio was known to the general, so he advanced to the door and was admitted. He returned in a short time with General Garcia, who greeted me cordially and asked me to enter with my assistente. The general introduced me to his staff — all in clean white uniforms and wearing side arms — and explained that the delay was caused by the necessary scrutiny of my credentials from the Cuban junta at Jamaica, which Gervacio had delivered to him.

There is humor in everything. I had been described in letters from the junta as "a man of confidence." The translator had made me "a confidence man."

Following breakfast we proceeded to business. I explained to General Garcia that my errand was purely military in its character, although I had left the United States with diplomatic credentials; that the President and the War Department desired the latest information respecting the military situation in Eastern Cuba. (Two other officers had been sent to Central and Western Cuba, but they were unable to reach their objectives.) Among matters it was imperative for the United States to know were the positions occupied by the Spanish troops, the condition and number of the Spanish forces, the character of their officers; especially of their commanding officers; the morale of the Spanish troops; the topography of the country, both local and general; communications, especially the conditions of the roads; in short, any information which would enable the American general staff to lay out a campaign. Last, but by no means least, General Garcia's suggestions as to a plan of campaign, joint or separate, between the Cuban armies and the forces of the United States. Also I informed him, my government would be glad to receive the same information respecting the Cuban forces, or as much as the general saw fit to give. If not incompatible with his plans, I would like to accompany the Cuban forces in the field in such capacity as he might see fit to assign me.

General Garcia meditated for a moment and then withdrew with all the members of his staff excepting Colonel Garcia, his son, who remained with me. About three o'clock the general returned and said he had decided to send three officers to the United States with me. These officers were men who had passed their lives in Cuba; were trained and tried; all knew the country, and in their particular capacities could answer all questions likely to be propounded. Were I to remain months in Cuba I might not be able to make so complete a report, and as time was the important element, the quicker the United States government got the information the better it would be for all concerned.

He went on to explain that his men needed arms, especially artillery, important in assaulting blockhouses. In ammunition he was very short, and the many rifles of varied calibre used made it difficult to get an ample supply. He thought it might be better to re-arm his men with American rifles in order to simplify that question.

General Collazo, a noted figure; Colonel Hernandez and Doctor Vieta, a valued relative who was familiar with the diseases of the island and the tropics generally, and two sailors, both familiar with the north coast, would go with us; they might be useful on the return expedition in case the United States should decide to furnish the supplies he wanted.

Could I proceed that day — hoy mismo?

Could I ask more?

Could I ask more? I had been continuously on the move for nine days in all kinds and conditions of terrain. I would have liked to have had a chance to look around me in these strange surroundings, but my answer was as prompt as his question. I simply replied: "Yes sir!"

Why not? General Garcia by his quick conception and speedy acceptance of conditions had saved me months of useless toil and had given my country the means of obtaining as minute information of the existing situation in the island as that possessed by the Cubans themselves; certainly as good as the enemy had.

For the next two hours I was the recipient of an informal reception. Then a final meal was served at five o'clock, and at its conclusion I was told that my escort was at the door. When I reached the street I was surprised not to see my former guide and companion in the column. I asked for Gervacio, and he and the others of the contingent from Jamaica came out. Gervacio wanted to go with me, but Garcia was adamant; all were needed for service on the south coast and I was to return by the north. I expressed to the general my appreciation for the services of Gervacio and his crew, and the column drafted from the fastnesses of Sierra Maestra. After a real Latin embrace I broke away and mounted. Three cheers rang out as we galloped northward.

I had delivered my message to Garcia!

My journey to General Garcia had been fraught with many dangers, but it was, compared with my trip back to the United States, by far the more important, an innocent ramble through a fair country. Going in there had been little to contend with, for the voyage from Jamaica had been on pleasant waters, while on the way to the Cuban commander I had been well guarded and well guided. But war had been declared and the Spanish were alert. Their soldiers patrolled every mile of shore, their boats every bay and inlet, the great guns of their forts stood ready to speak in no uncertain tones to anyone violating the rules of warfare. To all intents and purposes I was a spy within the enemy lines! Discovery meant death with one's face to the wall. Nor had I thought of reckoning with the angry elements of sea and air, which soon were to convince me that success is not always a matter of fair sailing.

But the effort must be made and it must be successful, otherwise my mission had been fruitless. On the happy termination of it might depend, in a large measure, the carrying to victory of the war.

My companions shared with me the apprehensions that naturally arose, so it was with great caution that we proceeded across Cuba, northward, going around the Spanish position at Cauto-El-Embarcadero, head of navigation on that river, at least for gunboats, until we came to the bottle-shaped harbor of Manati, where, on the side opposite, a great fort, bristling with guns, guarded the entrance.

If only the Spanish soldiery had known of our presence! But perhaps the very audacity of our undertaking was our salvation. Who would have suspected that an enemy on a mission such as was ours, would select such a place from which to embark?

The boat in which we made the voyage was a cockleshell, "capacity 104 cubic feet." For sails we had gunnysacks, pieced together. For rations boiled beef and water. In this craft we were to sail, and we did sail, 150 miles due north to New Providence, Nassau Island. Think of putting to sea on hostile waters, patrolled by swift, well-armed lanchas, in a vessel like that!

But "needs be when the devil drives!" It was our only method of fulfilling the full measure of duty.

It was at once apparent that this boat would not hold the six of us, so Dr. Vieta was sent back to Bayamo with the escort and the horses, while five of us prepared to run the gauntlet of Spanish guns and outwit Spanish gunboats with a craft not much larger than a skiff and with sails of gunnysacks!

There was a storm raging at the time we had fixed upon for our departure and we could not venture on the water while the waves were rolling so fiercely. Yet even in waiting there was danger! It was the time of the full moon and should the clouds dissipate with the passing of the gale our presence might be detected.

But the fates were with us!

At 11 o'clock we embarked. With only five aboard the boat was well down in the water. The ragged clouds rushed like mad things across the face of the moon, alternately hiding and disclosing us, while four tugged at the oars and a fifth steered a course. We could not see the fort as we passed, and that perhaps was the reason we were not seen, but it required no great stretch of imagination to picture the frowning muzzles of the great guns and we toiled on, expecting at any moment to hear the boom of a cannon and the scream of a shot. Our little craft reeled and tossed like an eggshell and many times we were on the point of capsizing, but our sailors knew the course, our gunnysack sails stood the test and soon we were making headway "across the trackless green."

Weary with the unwonted toil and with nothing to break the monotony of riding first one wave crest and then another, I fell asleep sitting bold upright.

But not for long. An immense wave hit us, nearly filling our boat with water and almost capsizing us. From that time on there was no sleep for anyone. It was bail, bail, bail the long night through. Drenched with brine, weary and worn, we were glad enough to get a glimpse of the sun as it peered through the haze on the horizon.

"Un vapor, Senores!" (a steamer) cried the steersman.

A feeling of alarm agitated every heart. Suppose it should be a Spanish warship? That would mean short shrift for all of us.

"Dos vapores, tres vapores, Caramba! doce vapores!" cried the steersman, my companions echoing his cries.

Could it be the Spanish fleet?

But no, it was the battleships of Admiral Sampson, steaming eastward to attack San Juan del Puerto Rico!

We breathed easier!

All that day we broiled and bailed, bailed and broiled. Yet no one slept or relaxed his anxious outlook. Despite the presence of the United States warships a gunboat might have escaped their vigilance and if so might overtake and capture us. Night fell on five of the most tired men that ever lived. We were almost worn out with fatigue, but for us there could be no rest. With the darkness came the wind again and with the wind the mighty waves and again it was bail, bail, bail, to keep the little vessel afloat. It was with feelings of intense relief that on the next morning, May 7, at about 10 o'clock, we sighted the Curly Keys at the southern end of Andros Islands of the Bahamas group and right gladly did we land there for a brief rest.

That afternoon we overhauled a sponging schooner, with a crew of thirteen Negroes, who spoke some outlandish gibberish we did not understand, but sign language is universal, and soon we had made arrangements for a transfer. This schooner carried a litter of pigs for food and an accordion. I never want to hear an accordion again. Tired almost to the point of utter exhaustion, I vainly sought sleep but the shrill notes of that instrument prevented it.

Next afternoon we were captured by quarantine officials as we turned the east end of New Providence Island, and were incarcerated at Hog Island, the fiction of yellow fever in Cuba having given them the excuse.

But next day I got word to the American consul general, Mr. McLean, and on May 10 he arranged our release. May 11 the schooner Fearless drew near the wharf and we went aboard.

We had got in behind Florida Keys when luck deserted us. The wind went down and all day May 12 we lay becalmed, but at night a breeze came up and on the morning of May 13 we were in Key West.

That night we took a train for Tampa and there boarded a train for Washington.

We arrived on schedule time and I reported to Russel A. Alger, secretary of war, who heard my story and told me to report to General Miles, taking General Garcia's aids with me. After he had received my report General Miles wrote the secretary of war: "I also recommend that First Lieutenant Andrew S. Rowan, 19th U.S. Infantry, be made a lieutenant-colonel of one of the regiments of immunes. Lieutenant Rowan made a journey across Cuba, was with the insurgent army with Lieutenant-General Garcia, and brought most important and valuable information to the government. This was a most perilous undertaking, and in my judgment Lieutenant Rowan performed an act of heroism and cool daring that has rarely been excelled in the annals of warfare."

I attended a meeting of the cabinet a day or so after my return, in company with General Miles, and at the close I received President McKinley's congratulations and thanks for the manner in which I had communicated his wishes to General Garcia and for the value of the work.

"You have performed a very brave deed!" were his last words to me, and this was the first time it had occurred to me that I had done more than my simple duty, the duty of a soldier who: "Is not to reason why," but to obey his orders.

I had carried my message to Garcia.

Footnotes

1. (I quote from the newspapers of the day: "The Cuban generals say the arrival of Lieutenant Rowan aroused the greatest enthusiasm throughout the Cuban army. There was no notice of his coming and the first seen of Lieutenant Rowan was as he galloped up Calle Commercial, followed by the Cuban guides who accompanied him.")

How I Carried the Message to Garcia